30p

Write Away

Keeping in touch from fan mail to faxes

Viv Edwards
Illustrated by Jan Lewis

Contents

Dear Reader 3
Keeping in touch 4
Special occasions 6
Writing to penfriends 8
Just for fun 12
For your eyes only 14
Making your point 16
Finding out 18
Designing your letters 20
From start to finish 22
Addressing your letters 24
In the post 26
Stamps 28
Letter collection and delivery 30
The great postal adventure 32
High speed letters 34
Making your mark 36
Handwriting 38
What can handwriting tell you? 40
Printing 42
Letters from history, history from letters 44
Family history 46
Index, useful addresses and book list 48

A & C Black · London

For Mary, Ramón and Christiane

First published 1991
A & C Black (Publishers) Limited
35 Bedford Row, London WC1R 4JH

ISBN 0–7136–3468–5

© 1991 A & C Black (Publishers) Limited

A CIP catalogue record for this book
is available from the British Library.

Acknowledgements
Artwork by Jan Lewis.
Photographs pp. 4, 5, 28, 29, 30 by Maggie Murray; p. 42 Beamish; pp. 46 and 47 by kind permission of David Wyman and Viv Edwards.

Thanks to Dafydd, Ceri and Siân Morriss, Ravinder Goodwin, Kamala and Mira Katbamna, Tom Massey, Marie and Julia Sienkewicz, Matthew Smolensky, Toby and Hugo Pritchard, the Indianapolis Children's Museum and the children of Redlands Primary School Reading who helped produce this book.

Apart from any fair dealing for the purposes of research or private study, or criticism or review, as permitted under the Copyright, Designs and Patents Act, 1988, this publication may be reproduced, stored or transmitted, in any form or by any means, only with the prior permission in writing of the publishers, or in the case of reprographic reproduction in accordance with the terms of licences issued by the Copyright Licensing Agency. Inquiries concerning reproduction outside those terms should be sent to the publishers at the above named address.

Filmset by August Filmsetting, Haydock, St Helens
Printed and bound in Italy by Amadeus.

Dear Reader,

These days, when we can communicate directly by phone with people on the other side of the world as easily as if they lived next door to us, it is easy to think that letter-writing is an outdated form of communication. As the songwriter Sydney Carter once wrote:

> 'Never send my love a letter
> Phoning her is so much better.
> After six and all day Sunday
> When the rate is cheaper.'

But letters and phone calls are very different kinds of communication. Phone conversations are quick and convenient. Letters are a permanent record. Sending invitations, saying thank you, keeping in touch with friends and relatives, telling famous people why you like them, making friends with people in other countries, sharing a joke or secret, making your views known, finding out . . . these are just some of the reasons for writing letters. When we write them, we can take our time to think of the best way of expressing what we want to say. And when we receive letters we can read them as many times as we want to, perhaps to check that we have understood everything, or simply to enjoy what the writer has to say.

Letter-writing is an important link with the past and the future. Old letters give us clues about the people who wrote them, and help us to understand what their lives were like. In the same way, people in the future, reading the letters you have written will be able to find out about you and your life.

WRITE AWAY is all about letter-writing. It's got ideas to help you write and design your own letters. It looks at the ways we send and receive letters. And it talks about what you'll need to get started, whether it's paper, pens and ink or a word processor.

Letters can be short or long, formal or friendly, plain or carefully designed and illustrated. Most important of all, they should be fun to write and enjoyable to receive.

Don't forget! Someone somewhere wants a letter from you. So read WRITE AWAY and write away!

Viv Edwards

Keeping in touch

Do your grandparents or other relatives live too far away for you to visit each other regularly? Or perhaps a good friend has moved away to another town or even to another country. Maybe you know someone who finds it difficult to get out of the house because he or she is elderly or ill. If you think about it, there are probably lots of people who would be very happy to get a letter from you.

Having a chat

Writing to someone you know well should be very much like having a conversation with them. There are no rules about the length of your letters; they can be as long or as short as you like. When you write, you may like to think about using some – or all – of these ideas

* The most important things that have been happening to you and your family. What's new since you last met or wrote?
* News about people you both know.
* Good jokes you've heard.

✷ Feelings and opinions about books you've read, television programmes you've seen or world events.

✷ Don't forget to ask questions about what has been happening to the person you are writing to.

✷ Do you have a recent photo of yourself that you can send?

P.S. If you forget to say something in the letter, you can add a *P.S.* or *postscript* (from the Latin *post* – after; *scribere* – to write.)

P.P.S. If you remember something else when you have written your P.S., you can add a P.P.S. (a post postscript!)

Apart from letters...

...there are other ways of keeping in touch. You can show that you are thinking of someone by sending them a postcard when you're on holiday or a greetings card on special occasions like their birthday and Christmas. You could also record your letter and send it in the form of a cassette.

Special occasions

Invitations

Something special happening at school? Your birthday? Christmas? New Year? Saying goodbye to a friend who is going away? There are all sorts of reasons for inviting people to a party or special event. Of course you could invite your guests by phone, but sending a written invitation makes the occasion much more special.

It is possible to buy ready-printed invitations in all sorts of styles and for lots of different occasions. But have you ever thought of making your own? Here are some ideas to start you thinking.

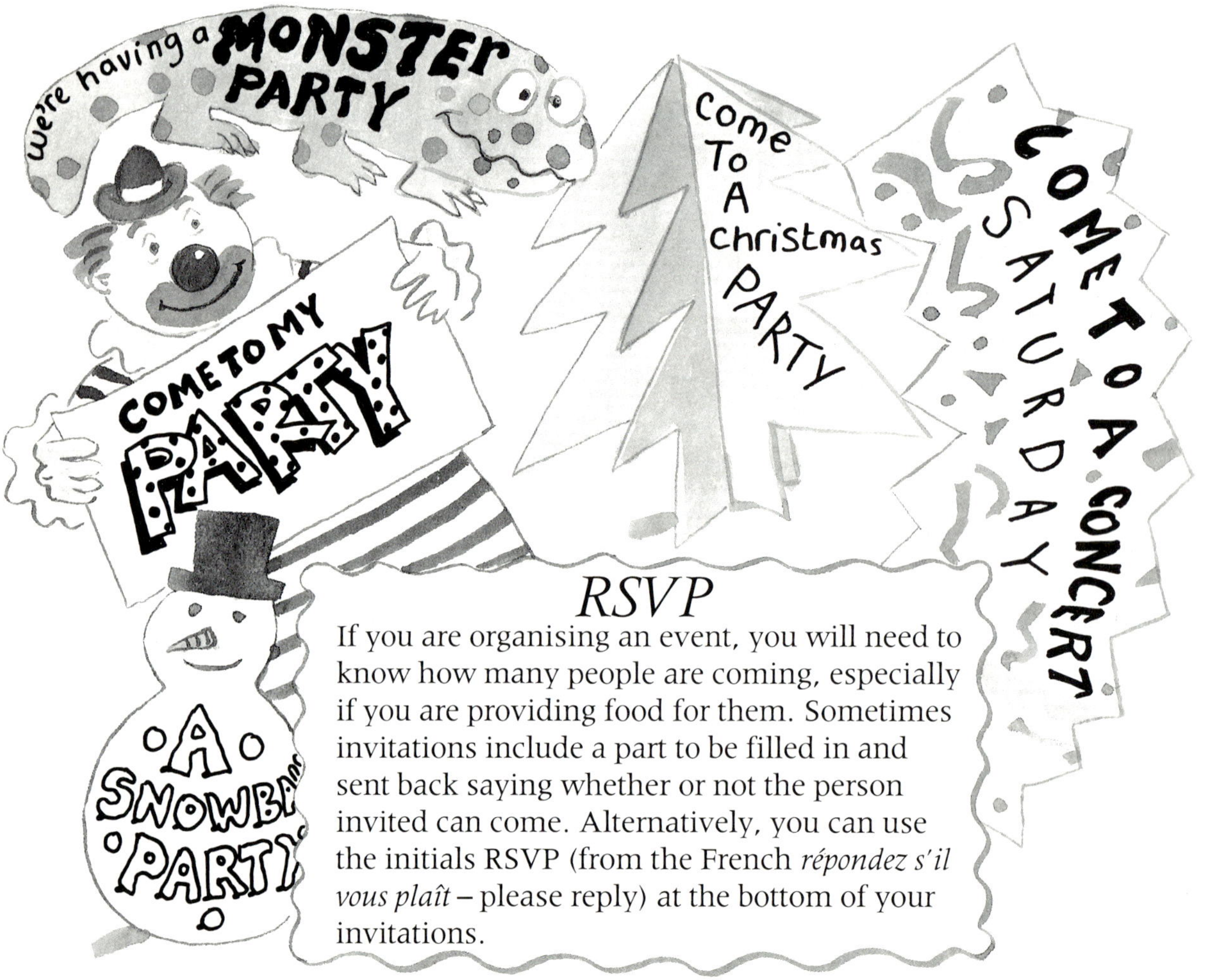

RSVP

If you are organising an event, you will need to know how many people are coming, especially if you are providing food for them. Sometimes invitations include a part to be filled in and sent back saying whether or not the person invited can come. Alternatively, you can use the initials RSVP (from the French *répondez s'il vous plaît* – please reply) at the bottom of your invitations.

Saying thankyou

Perhaps the kind of letter that you will write most frequently will be to relatives and friends who have sent you presents. After all, if someone has taken the time to choose, wrap and sent you a present, it is only fair for them to receive a thankyou letter in return!

Sometimes you may be thrilled with the presents you've received, but less enthusiastic when it comes to putting pen to paper to say thanks. But there are all sorts of ways of making thankyou letters fun to write.

> 3 The drive
> Edinburgh E35LT
> Tuesday, Sept. 1st
>
> Dear Uncle John,
> You were right! A gift voucher WAS what I really wanted! I used it to buy some new pens and stationery and you are the first to benefit from these new purchases!
>
> I had a very good birthday. I thought I would have to till christmas for a new computer. You can imagine how pleased I was to find I had it for my Birthday instead. You can play some games on it when you come to see us next, but if you want to beat me you'll have to start practising now

> 1 Blenheim Road,
> Gargrave LS41 3TU
>
> Friday, April 4th
>
> Dear Granny,
> What a fantastic weekend! I enjoyed it all from beginning to end. The best bit was when we went down to the river. There was so much going on there and wasn't it funny when that man tripped over his dog and fell in? Good job he could swim!
> Anyway, thanks very much for giving me such a nice time. It won't be long before you come to see us at half term.
>
> Lots of love,
> Tom.

* You could make your thankyou letters more interesting by adding illustrations or using stickers.

* If your handwriting is not too good, perhaps you could use a typewriter or a word processor if you have one at home.

* If you have a lot of thankyou letters to write, you may prefer to write one very good letter and make photocopies of it, or print out copies from a word processor, but of course this is far less personal. You could try personalising the copies by adding a special hand-written message to each one, or by decorating them differently.

Writing to penfriends

Letter-writing is an excellent way of making friends. When you write to a penfriend, even though you may never have met, you have the chance to get to know another person and find out all about each other.

How to find penfriends

If you decide that you would like to have a penfriend, how do you go about finding one? Some of the main penfriend organizations are listed in the address section at the back of this book. Whichever organization you choose will try to match you up with a suitable penfriend. In order to do this they will need to know:

* Your name.
* Your age.
* Whether you are a girl or a boy.
* If you want to write to a boy or a girl or if you don't mind.
* Your main interests.
* Where you would like your penfriend to come from.
* Which language you want to write in.

[Pages 19, 30 and 31 of this book include information you'll need about how to send letters abroad.]

Would you make a good penfriend?

Some people make better penfriends than others. So how do you know if writing to a penfriend is the right hobby for *you* to take up?

Answer the questions below as honestly as you can. When you have finished, look at the key on page 48 and work out your score.

1 Do you enjoy getting letters
a very much?
b quite alot?
c not at all?

2 Do you write thankyou letters for Christmas and birthday presents
a without anyone telling you that you should?
b with a little encouragement?
c only when someone threatens you with terrible consequences if you don't?

3 If you are away from home for two weeks would you
a write at least one letter?
b send a postcard?
c tell everybody about what happened when you get back?

4 Are you the sort of person who, when something needs to be done
a does it immediately?
b gets round to it fairly quickly?
c puts it off for as long as is humanly possible?

5 Are you somebody who finds new places and new ideas
a very exciting?
b quite exciting?
c not particularly exciting?

6 Do you like collecting and exchanging things like stamps and postcards
a very much?
b quite a lot?
c not at all?

7 When you hear other languages and dialects, do you
a want to learn how to speak like that yourself?
b enjoy listening?
c think if would be better if everybody spoke like you?

Writing to someone you know is easy. Writing to someone you don't know can be trickier, at least at the beginning, because it's sometimes difficult to know where to start.

* First of all, you will need to find out certain basic information about each other – how old are you? what do you look like? (sending a photograph is an easy way to handle this one.) What do you like doing? How many people are there in your family? Who are they and what are they like?

* As the correspondence grows, you can talk about what you do at school and how you spend your day. It is astonishing how different this can be from one country to another, and even sometimes within the same country.

* Write about interesting places you have visited or things you have done.

* Talk about things that are important to you in the same way as you would if you were talking to an 'ordinary' friend.

* Remember that letter-writing should be like conversation; it shouldn't be one-sided. Ask questions and reply to the ones your penfriend asks you.

* You can add to the interest of your letters in all sorts of other ways, too. Photographs, drawings, newspaper cuttings, bus tickets, postcards and stamps can easily be slipped into a letter and records, tapes and magazines can be sent quite cheaply by surface mail.

* Don't forget, penfriendships are very much like any other kind of friendship; some work and some don't. So don't be discouraged if your first attempt wasn't a success. Try again!

Spectacular penfriendships!

The message in a bottle

In 1970, a ten year old English girl called Jane Lancaster, on holiday in Spain, put her name and address in a bottle and threw it out to sea. The bottle was spotted some weeks later by the Vuillaume family on holiday in the south of France. They put the sea-stained paper away in a drawer and forgot about it.

Five years later, the Vuillaumes were moving house, and as they emptied the drawer, they found the message again. This time they decided to write to the Lancasters. Now both families are firm friends. They have visited each other often and still write regularly.

Faithful friends!

The longest-lasting penfriends were Mrs Ida McDougall of Tasmania, Australia and Miss R. Norton of Sevenoaks, Kent. They wrote to each other for 75 years, from 1904 until Mrs McDougall died in 1979.

Just for fun

My grandfather once wrote to me asking for some advice. He said he had been offered a job sandpapering down elephants into greyhounds and wanted to know if I thought he should accept. This was when I realised that letters don't always have to have a serious purpose. Sometimes they can be just for fun.

When it's no joke

Of course, there is always the possibility that a joke will go too far. Take the story of Buddy. One day in 1982, Cameron Black picked up a message over his CB radio that an eight year-old boy was dying of cancer. The boy's last wish was to appear in the Guiness Book of Records for receiving the largest ever number of postcards. Mr Black offered his own post office box in Paisley, Scotland as a mailing address.

Soon afterwards, postcards began flooding in at the rate of 20,000 a day. The President of the United States sent a letter; several international airlines put out a message about Buddy on their global telex networks; newspapers and television companies all over the world organised appeals on Buddy's behalf.

But when Mr Black tried to find out where Buddy lived, he started to become very suspicious. He contacted schools and hospitals all over Scotland without any success. In the meantime, postal workers were trying to cope with huge piles of mail for Buddy – until it became clear that Buddy didn't exist. This is one 'joke' that really went too far.

Chain letters

Have you every received a chain letter? Chain letters usually list the names of five or six people. They tell you to write to the person at the top of the list, cross this person's name off and put your own name at the bottom. You then send a letter with the new list to several other people. The promise is that, within a short time, as you reach the top of the list, you will receive hundreds of postcards, gifts or letters.

The arithmetic of chain letters is interesting. If there are five names on the letter, and no breaks in the chain, it would only take 11 steps to cover the whole population of the United States.

Chain letters

step		
1	5×5 =	25
2	25×5 =	125
3	125×5 =	625
4	625×5 =	3,125
5	3,125×5 =	15,625
6	15,625×5 =	78,125
7	78,125×5 =	390,625
8	390,625×5 =	1,953,125
9	1,953,125×5 =	9,765,625
10	9,765,625×5 =	48,828,125
11	48,828,125×5	244,140,625!

At first, chain letters sound as if they might be fun, but beware! They hardly ever work because many people don't bother to reply and sometimes they can be frightening. Some ask for money. Some make threats like 'If you break this chain you will have bad luck for the next ten years'. The best thing to do with letters of this kind is to throw them away.

For your eyes only

Code letters

If you have a secret to tell someone, you could send it written in a code that you've agreed with that person, so that if anyone else reads your message, they won't be able to understand it.

There are countless different codes that you can use for writing. Some of the simplest ones work by changing letters into numbers. For instance, if there are 26 letters in the alphabet, they can each be numbered from one to 26.

Code letters

A 1 B 2 C 3 D 4 E 5 F 6
G 7 H 8 I 9 J 10 K 11 L 12
M 13 N 14 O 15 P 16 Q 17 R 18
S 19 T 20 U 21 V 22 W 23 X 24
Y 25 Z 26

When you write messages using this code, put a stroke between each number:

What does this message say? Turn to page 48 for the answer.

3/15/4/5 12/5/20/20/5/18/19 18/21/12/5 15/11 !

Another system is to use thirteen numbers or symbols with a dot either above or below them:

A B C D E F G H I J K L M
0 1 2 3 4 5 6 7 8 9 ! ? [ ]
N O P Q R S T U V W X Y Z

Can you use this code to write **EMERGENCY SUBJECT BEING TAILED** Turn to page 48 to check your message.

If you think that even your pet goldfish could break these codes, start working on your own systems.

Mirror writing

Another way to throw people off your trail is to use mirror writing. Write out the message you want to send on a piece of paper. Hold the message up to a mirror, then copy from the mirror onto a second piece of paper.

I USED TO SEE DOUBLE BUT NOW...

↑ place mirror here

Invisible writing

The last word in secrecy is of course, the letter written in invisible ink! Write an ordinary letter which includes a codeword that you have agreed on with your friend. This will warn them that they should be on the lookout for an invisible message. Then write between the lines or on the back of the letter. You can use:

* Wax from a candle. To read the message, sprinkle the paper with chalk dust and then shake it off. The chalk only sticks to the wax.

* A sharpened matchstick, or a pen that doesn't work, dipped in apple or lemon juice. Heat the paper in a cool oven (250°F, Gas Mark 2) for a short time and the juice will darken.

* A sharpened, dampened matchstick. When you want to read the message, brush the paper with a watery ink and the writing will show up slightly darker.

Making your point

Some people get angry about cruelty to animals or pollution; others worry about the threat of war or road safety. Is there anything you feel very strongly about?

Save the whale

Whales are an endangered species and, if hunting continues, they will soon be extinct. At a public ceremony in December 1985, Jose Sarney, the President of Brazil, signed a decree forbidding whaling in Brazilian waters for the next five years. At the ceremony, the President said that he had been deeply moved by the thousands of letters from children all over Brazil asking him to end the whale killings.

Cry freedom!

The activities of Amnesty International have shown very clearly how effective letters can be in making people – and even governments – change their minds. Amnesty has branches and members all over the world. The organization runs many campaigns on behalf of people who have been put in prison for their political or religious beliefs. For instance, Alfonso's mother was a journalist who was put in jail for telling the truth about what was happening in her country, El Salvador. To protect Alfonso from government death squads, his grandmother kept him indoors for over two years. However, after thousands of letters from Amnesty International members all over the world appealing against this injustice, Alfonso and his mother have now been freed.

If you have a strong opinion about something, why not write a letter? You might not succeed in changing the world, but at least you will have the satisfaction of telling those responsible how you feel.

When not to write

Have you ever had a day when everything goes wrong? An important part is missing from your new game. You open a packet of biscuits and find them all stuck together. The seam on your new sweatshirt comes undone. You are all set to put pen to paper and tell the manufacturers what you think of them. But wait . . . this may be one situation when writing a letter of complaint would not be the best thing to do.

Food wrappers usually have an address printed on them to which you can write if you are not satisfied with the goods. But in most cases, if you have bought something which does not work or doesn't match the description on the packaging, you should deal directly with the store where you bought it and not the manufacturer.

Usually it is quicker if you can discuss things face to face. As soon as possible, take the item back to the shop, together with your receipt or proof of purchase and explain what is wrong. When you are making a reasonable complaint, most stores will be happy to give you a replacement, reduce the price or give you your money back.

If the store cannot help and you are still not satisfied, a consumer adviser such as the Citizen's Advice Bureau will often be able to help you. Ask at your local library where to find them, or look up their address and phone number in the telephone directory.

By the way

Be polite.
Don't get carried away!

Finding out
Fan letters

Is there someone you admire more than anyone else? Your favourite author? A rock star? An actor? Someone in public life? Have you ever thought of writing to them?

Some singers, actors and musicians are so well liked that they have special fan clubs. You will find the addresses in music magazines and publications aimed at young people. You can join a fan club as a way of getting autographs, photos, news and other information about your favourite star.

Letters will usually reach an actor if you sent them to the television company where you have seen them work most recently or to the theatre where he or she is performing. If you particularly like an author, you can write to him or her at the address of the publisher that you will find on the inside of their book.

---

19 Lambourne Way,
Leeds LS21 7HH
Friday, March 21st

Dear Andy,
I think you do a really good job of presenting children's T.V programmes. Nearly everybody else on children's T.V is white and I think it is about time we had more black personalities like you.
I would like to be a journalist or a T.V reporter when I grow up. How did you get started on T.V?

Yours sincerely
Jessy Hall.

---

12 Pitt Road
Belfast BT5 5JG
September 1st

Dear Judy Blume,
I just finished reading Superfudge. I thought it was great. In fact, Fudge is so much like my own brother I think you must have based it on him! Lots of people think he's very funny, but I think he's a pain. How long does it take you to write your books?
And do you base your characters on people you know or do you just make them up? If you have time to write

---

14 Star Lane
Brighton BN2
October 29th

Dear Cliff,
All my friends make fun of me because I think you're great. They say only mothers and grannies like your music. Anyway, I don't care. I think your records make good listening and anyone who has hits for as long as you must be very special.
Best wishes
Jenny Piper

Information and freebies

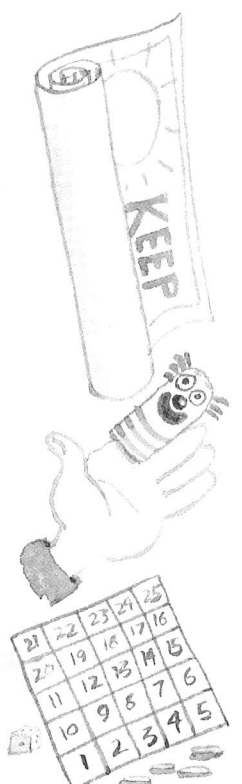

Writing letters is a very good way of finding out information on everything from travel and sport to conservation and craft. Look out for food packages, toy wrappers, books and magazines that tell you about special offers. Very often these are free or involve only a very small charge. Many charities, clubs, companies and organizations supply 'freebies' in the form of games, posters, maps, badges or books which publicize the work they do.

If you want information about a particular organization, ask for help at your local library in finding their address. Or have a look through the book *Free Stuff for Kids* (Exley Publications) which gives details of hundreds of things to send away for.

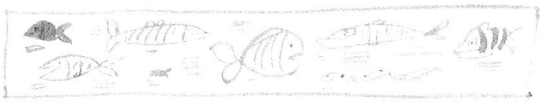

Sending a stamped addressed envelope (s.a.e.)

You are more likely to receive a rapid reply when writing away for information if you enclose a stamped addressed envelope. Some special offers also ask you to send a s.a.e. with your request.

In most cases you can send an ordinary small envelope, but if you are asked to enclose a 'large envelope' you should use one which measures at least 6" by 9" (15 cm by 23 cm.) An 'extra large envelope' will measure at least 9" by 12" (23 cm by 31 cm.)

✱ Write your letter clearly, stating your name, address, the date and why you are writing.

✱ Write your own address on an envelope and put a stamp on it.

✱ Fold the stamped addressed envelope and put it with your letter in another envelope.

✱ Address the second envelope to the company or organization. Don't forget to put a stamp on this envelope too.

Writing abroad

If you are writing abroad for information from another country, you'll need to buy an international reply coupon from your post office. The person who receives your letter will then be able to exchange the coupon for stamps at their own post office. If you want to receive you reply by air mail you will need to send two coupons; otherwise one will do.

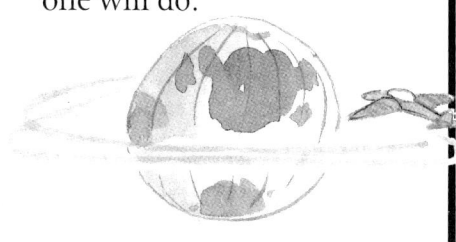

Designing your letters

When you write a letter, you are trying to put across a message, and the way you design your letter is very important if your message is to be communicated successfully.

The paper you choose, the way you lay things out, what you say and how you say it: all these things will depend on whether you are writing an informal letter to a friend or somebody you know well, or a formal letter to someone you may never have met.

The same kind of rules guide how you set out your letter. Your best friend already knows your full name and address. Building Society managers, on the other hand, have lots of customers and probably don't know you personally. They need to be able to find out important information about the people writing to them at a glance, and there are certain ways of providing this information.

This part of **Write Away** will show you how to plan your letters and how to lay them out. It will give you some ideas for designing and decorating letters to family and friends. And it will talk about the things you need to think about if you want to make a good impression when you are writing serious letters.

Letters to friends

'Fourwinds'
The green,
New town,
XYZ 120
March 19th

When you write an informal letter to a friend, there are no hard and fast rules about how to set out your letter and what information needs to be included. You can have a lot of fun designing it too. Letters can be good to look at as well as interesting to read.

You can put your address in one of a number of positions, you can shorten it or even leave it out altogether.

The way you position the letter on the page can be quite important. To create the best visual effect, margins should be neither too small, nor too large.

Have fun designing your own margins, decorating your letters with stickers or making special designs for special occasions.

love,
Jane
x

P.S have you heard the one about the.....

From start to finish

Rough drafts

When you are writing a formal letter, possibly to someone you have never met, you need to think carefully what you are going to say. If you want to be taken seriously and to make a good impression, take time composing your letter. Make a rough draft first. For example, imagine you'd bought a box of chocolates, and discovered when you got home that they were mouldy. Your rough draft of a letter to the manufacturer might look like this:

> 2. Says on the box that if you have a complaint to write to the company with proof of purchase
> 3. I'm sending the wrapper.
> 1. Chocolates were mouldy and stuck together.
> 4. Want my money back or another box of mints.

When you're planning a formal letter,

* Write down all the points you want to make.
* Number them in the order that you want to include them in your letter.
* Write out a rough copy first. Does it say everything you want it to?
* Ask somebody else to read it. What do they think?
* Check your spelling in a dictionary, or by using the spell function if you are composing your letter on a word processor, or ask an adult for some help.
* If you are happy with your letter, copy it out clearly.

Setting it out

If you are writing a formal letter there are a few simples rules which help the reader find out information more easily.

> Put the name and address of the person you are writing to on the left hand side of the paper, a little lower down.

> Put your address and postcode on the right hand side of the page, with the date underneath.

> The Director,
> Consumer services
> The Chocolate Box Co. Ltd.
> 14 South Way
> Cardiff CF1 8HG
>
> 18 Morgan rd.
> Ferndale,
> Avon. BS2 7HH
> March 31st 1991
>
> Dear Sir or Madam,
> I recently bought a box of your chocolate mints. When I opened them, they were covered in a white mould and all stuck together.
> It says on the packet that, in case of complaint, customers should write to you with proof of purchase. I am enclosing the wrapper from the chocolate mints.
> I would be grateful if you would either refund my money or send me another box of chocolate mints.
> Yours faithfully
> Mira Katbamna
> MIRA KATBAMNA (miss)

> Write on plain paper, preferably white. You are unlikely to be taken very seriously if your writing paper has cartoon characters or other designs on it!

> It's a good idea to print your name under your signature to make sure the reader will understand it. It is also helpful to put *Mr., Miss or Ms.* in brackets afterwards so that they will know how to address you when they reply.

If you don't know the name of the person you're writing to, or whether they are male or female, start your letter with *Dear Sir or Madam*. If you do know their name, you can put *Dear Mr...* or *Mrs...* or *Miss...* or *Ms...*

If you use *'Dear Sir or Madam'*, and end your letter *'Yours faithfully'*. If you use the person's name, end with *'Yours sincerely'*.

Addressing your letters

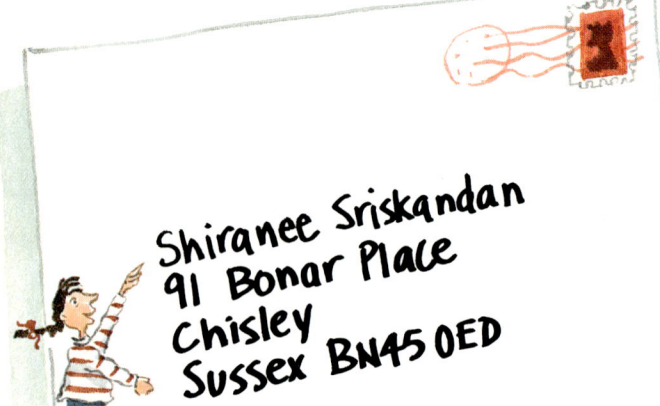

Start the address about a third of the way down the envelope. If you write any further up there may not be enough room for the stamps or part of the address may be covered by the postmark.

It's a good idea to put your own address on the back of the envelope. Then, if the person you are writing to has moved or if the address is incorrect, the post office can send the letter back to you.

The long and the short of it

Addresses vary greatly in length from one country to another. The British, for example, are very fond of long addresses. In other countries, the post office often manages to deliver letters with very much less information!

Mr Dafydd Morriss
'Homelea'
16 Patrick Road
Littlewick Green,
Nr Cardiff,
Mid-Glamorgan, CF5 3AB
WALES

LE TEXIER Marie,
35120 Laille,
FRANCE

The longest place name in the world now in use is

Taumatawhakatangihangakoauauotamateapokaiwhenuakitanatahu

It is the name of a hill in the Southern Hawke's Bay district of North Island, New Zealand.

Madame Dupont Marie
80 rue Corneille,
75006 Paris,
France

Mario Gabba
Via Fra Cristoforo
00195 ROMA
ITALY.

PJ Adlan
55 West 79th street
New York
N.Y. 10022
U.S.A

Some things to look out for:

✻ In some countries, people tend to put the family name before the first name on envelopes:

Mlle. CONORT Christiane

✻ In some countries, the house number comes before the name of the street; in others it comes afterwards:

6 Melrose Avenue

Alter Heidberg 12

✻ In many small towns and country districts, house numbers don't appear at all:

Bowling Alley Point, Nundle, NSW

✻ In some countries, postcodes are made up entirely of numbers, but in others they are made up of letters and numbers. Sometimes the postcodes come in front of the town; sometimes they are written after the town, state or province:

Arizona 85721

1024 LK Amsterdam

In the post

There is a lot more to sending and receiving letters than you might at first think. For example, did you know that:

A seven-year-old girl wrote one of the shortest ever letters to be published in a newspaper. The girl was replying to an earlier letter in *The Times* about people called Kerenhappuch. She simply wrote 'Sir, Yours faithfully, Caroline Sophia Kerenhappuch Parkes'.

The same birthday card was sent to and from Mrs Amelia Finch of Lakehurst, New Jersey, USA and Mr Paul Warburgh of Huntingdon, New York every year from 1st February 1927 to 18 April 1980.

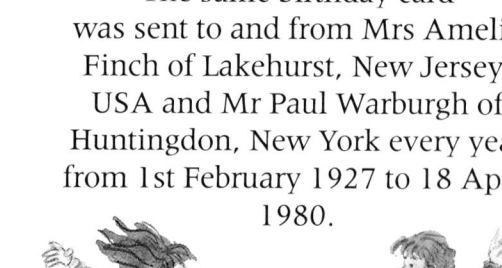

The shortest recorded correspondence took place in 1892 between the French writer Victor Hugo and his publisher, Hurst and Blackett. Hugo was wondering how well his new book, *Les Misérables*, was selling, and wrote '?'. The publisher replied, '!'

The longest letter was 1,402,344 words long and was written by Alan Foreman of Erith, Kent, England to his wife. He started writing it on 3rd January 1982 and finally posted it on 25th Janaury 1984.

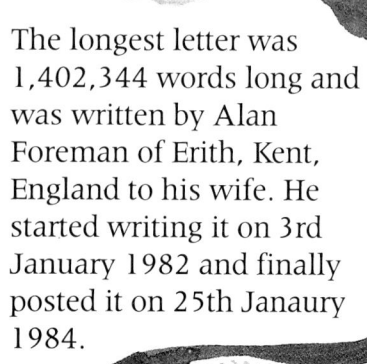

The busiest postal service in the world is the United States Postal Service. In 1985, it handled 140.1 billion letters and packages. The average number of letters posted by each person during this period was 589.

American baseball star, Hank Aaron, received 900,000 letters in 1974. He is the current holder of the record for the highest number of letters received by a private individual in one year.

An unsuccessful experiment was launched in Liege, Belgium in 1879. Thirty-seven cats were supposed to carry mail to villages within a thirty kilometre radius of the city centre. The experiment failed because the cats tended to wander off in all directions.

James Sturrock was convalescing in a Swiss hospital after a battle injury in the First World War. On 20th September 1916, he sent a postcard to his son in Perth, Scotland. Unfortunately it fell behind a counter and was only discovered when the sorting office was refitted. Mr Sturrock's son, Edwin, finally received the postcard on 19th May 1975, almost sixty years later.

One of the most unusual letter boxes ever was the Whalers' Tree at Still Harbour near Cape Horn. Ships would stop to pick up mail left among the tree roots. Letters took from fourteen months to two years to reach their destination.

Have you ever looked closely at the stamps and postmarks on the letters you receive? Have you ever thought about what happens to letters after you post them? Want to know more? Then read on!

Stamps

If you write and receive letters frequently, you could think about starting a collection of stamps and postmarks. And if you are already a keen collector, the stamps on the letters you receive will be an added bonus. Even if you don't particularly enjoy collecting things, you can still enjoy looking at the different kinds of stamps, postmarks, stickers and markings which you will find on the envelopes you receive. Try to put interesting stamps on your own envelopes. This can be fun both for you and for the person receiving the letter.

There are three main kinds of stamp:

Definitives
Definitives are the 'everyday stamps' of a country and usually stay in circulation for a number of years. Often the same stamp is issued in different colours for different prices.

Commemoratives
Commemoratives are issued for a limited period of time in honour of a special event which is represented on the stamp.

Special issues
Special issues are also issued for a limited period but are not tied to a particular event.

Franking machines and postmarks

The stamps you use on envelopes are cancelled with postmarks so that they cannot be used again. Postmarks usually show the name and postcode of the place where the letter was posted, as well as the date and time. You often find slogans advertising an event or a place next to the postmark.

Not all letters have stamps on their envelopes. Some organizations which send out large mailings pre-print the postmark on the envelopes. Others have special franking machines which print the amount of postage due as well as the postmark. The machine records these amounts and the user pays the post office direct instead of buying stamps.

Letter collection and delivery

Sending mail

There are various ways to send your letters. The price depends on the weight, the country of destination and the service that you choose. The post office can give you the help you need and will often have leaflets describing the different services they offer.

 US
 Canada
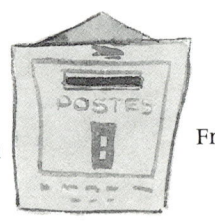 France
 UK

Air mail

Air mail services operate over long distances. This is the quickest but also the most expensive way of sending letters and parcels. Some countries have special air mail stamps. These are usually countries which transport some of their internal mail by air. Other countries use air mail labels. These are usually blue and have the French words *par avion* (by plane) printed on them, with the equivalent words in the national language.

Most countries also have aerogrammes, special lightweight letter sheets, often with a stamp printed on them. Because they are so light, they cost less than an ordinary letter to send. But be careful not to put anything inside, or to put tape or stickers on the outside, or you will have to pay the full rate.

Surface mail

Letters and parcels sent by surface mail travel by road, rail and when necessary, sea. For short distances, letters will automatically go by surface mail. For long distances, surface letters take longer but cost less.

Watch out!

Some organizations are prepared to pay the postage on your letters; you simply write FREEPOST in the address and you don't have to buy a stamp. Most letters though, need stamps. If you forget, the post man or woman will ask the person receiving the letter to pay twice the value of the stamp which you should have put on the envelope.

Receiving mail

There are also lots of different systems for receiving letters. Some people have their letters delivered to special boxes at the post office. They have a key to the box and go there to collect their mail in person.

Siân Morriss, PO Box 86, Glasgow G1 1AA

If you want to be able to receive mail when you are on holiday, but don't know where you will be staying, you can ask friends to write to you at the *Poste Restante* in a town you know you will be passing through. You can simply call at the post office to find out whether any letters have arrived for you.

Kamala Katbamna, Poste Restante, Newquay, Cornwall

In the United Kingdom, every house has a letter box in the front door. Unfortunately, letter boxes are not always placed in convenient positions and sometimes they are too small for large envelopes or parcels.

In most countries, letters are delivered to post boxes outside the house. This saves the post man or woman a lot of walking and bending! Outside boxes have other advantages, too. If people have letters ready to send, they put a special sign up on their boxes and the post man or woman takes it back to the post office for them.

The great postal adventure

What happens to a letter when you post it? Writing a letter is just the start of a fascinating and complex process.

1 Ceri lives in Reading, a large town in England. He often writes to his friend, Matthew, who lives in Monmouth, Illinois, a small town in the midwest of America.

2 Ceri posts his letter to Matthew at 5 p.m. The postman or woman collects it from the letter box and takes it to the sorting office at the main post office.

3 Letters to destinations overseas are sorted by hand. Letters for the midwest of America are taken by a van which leaves for Heathrow airport at 9.30 a.m. the next morning.

4 Ceri's letter is loaded on to British Airways flight 297 which takes off for Chicago at 14.15 p.m. that afternoon. It arrives at O'Hare airport ten hours later.

5 The letter is taken by road to the area Distribution Center.

6 The next day, it goes by road to the regional office in Galesburg. It is sorted there by hand before going by road again to the post office in Monmouth. There, every house in Monmouth has its own 'pigeon hole'. Ceri's letter is sorted into Matthew's pigeon hole.

7 Five thousand miles and three days later, the postman or woman delivers the letter to Matthew.

8 Now it's Matthew's turn to write and the great postal adventure will start all over again!

High speed letters

Fax machines

The postal service is no longer the only way to send letters. When it is important for a document to reach its destination quickly the best solution is often to fax it through the telephone network.

The name fax comes from *facsimile*, a Latin word meaning an exact copy. A document is placed in the fax machine which converts patterns of light and dark into sound signals and sends them along the phone lines via a piece of electronic equipment called a modem. On the receiving end, similar equipment converts the incoming signals into marks on a sheet of heat-sensitive paper and then produces a photocopy. It takes about 20 seconds to transmit a page of black print and about two minutes to transmit a picture with lots of different tones or shades of grey.

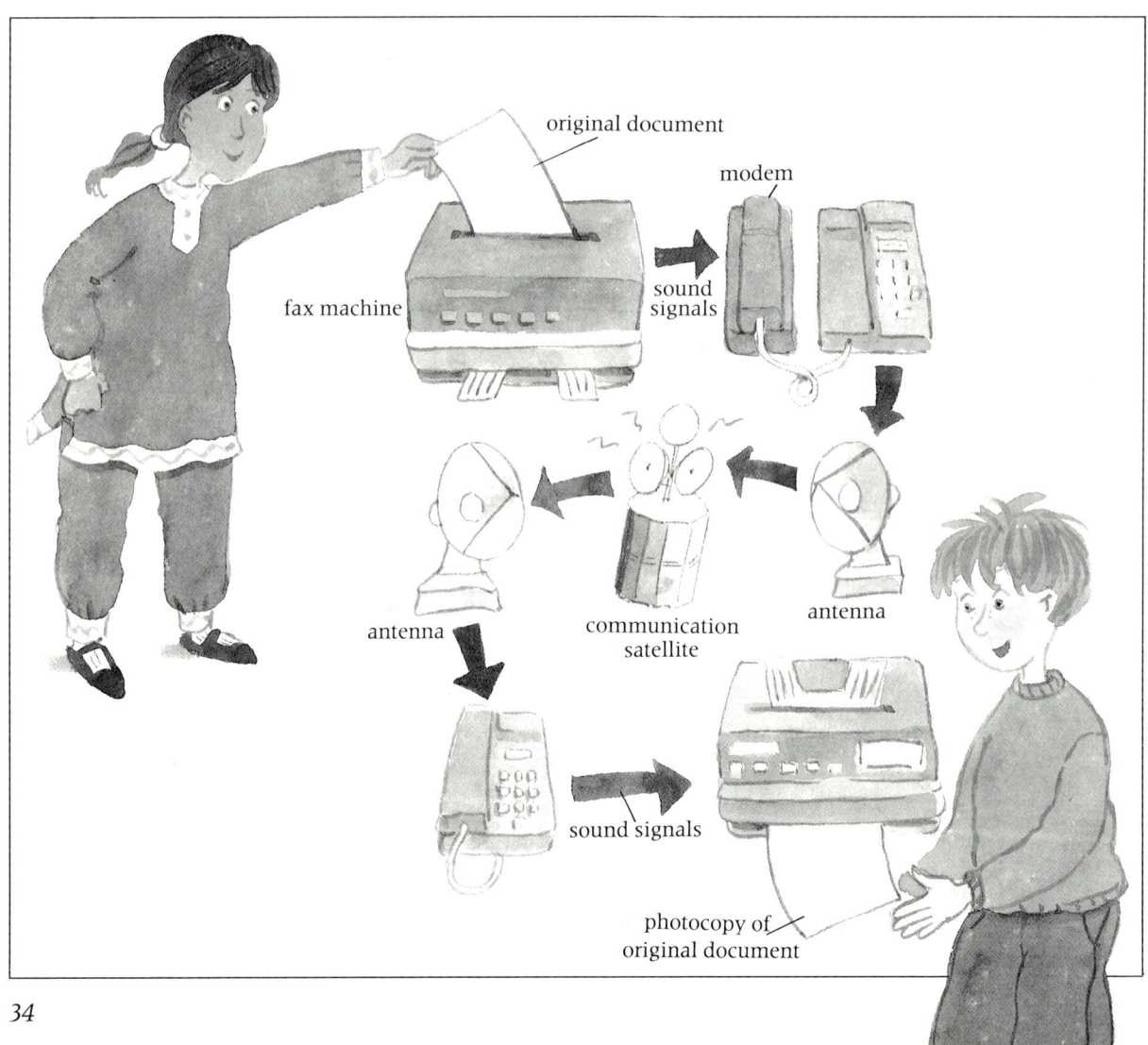

E-mail

It is also possible to use a modem to connect a personal computer to the telephone lines. As part of the electronic mail or e-mail network, you can send and receive messages from all over the world. In the early days, e-mail was used mainly by businesses, but gradually it is spreading to schools, colleges and private individuals.

E-mail has been used in classrooms to link school children not only in the same country but all over the world. When schools are part of a computer network, children in Britain who want to know what it's like to live in Tasmania, for example, can find out directly from people living there. Whereas it would take well over a week to send a letter to Tasmania and receive the reply, e-mail letters travel the same distance in minutes.

Making your mark

There are all sorts of reasons for writing letters and many different ways of designing and laying them out. The paper you use will set the tone of your letter – whether it's intended to be lighthearted or serious. Your choice of pen can also be important in creating a particular impression or effect. And there's the question of handwriting – just how important is it and what can it tell people about you?

Paper

According to history, the earliest paper was made in China around AD 105. The Chinese kept their skills a closely-guarded secret, and it was only very slowly that the knowledge of paper-making spread to other parts of the world. It reached Italy and Spain in the 1100s and two hundred years later, paper began to be made in Britain.

There are hundreds of different substances which can be used to make paper. In the 1700s, a German clergyman called Dr Jacob Schaeffer experimented with almost 80 different paper-making materials including cabbages, beans and potatoes.

Most paper is made from wood. Many people are worried that forests are being cleared much faster than they can grow again. One solution is to recycle paper. This means that fewer trees will be felled. Recycled paper takes less energy to produce and so causes less pollution.

Paper can be bought in a variety of sizes. The standard for measurement is based on an area of one square metre and is called A1. This is then divided into a smaller area, half the size of A1 which is called A2. A3 is half the size of A2 and so on, down to A6.

Paper also comes in different weights. The weight of the paper you use is especially important when sending letters by air mail. If your letter weighs more than 10 grams, postage can be very expensive. However, you can buy special air mail paper which is very light indeed.

Pen and ink

Various different tools have been used for writing over the ages including the reed, the stylus, (from the Latin word *stilus*, meaning writing implement) made of ivory bone or metal, and the quill. Today, pens come in all sorts of shapes and sizes and they can be used to create many different effects.

Calligraphy pens

These are used for various kinds of decorative writing. They have metal nibs in several different sizes which you dip into ink. Some pens have square nibs which are good for italic writing. By holding the nib at different angles, you can produce a combination of thick and thin strokes.

Other calligraphy pens have round or square-shaped nibs which lie flat on the paper and give a constant stroke thickness.

Fibre and felt tip pens

These are available in many different point and nib shapes and were developed as part of the American space programme because astronauts needed to be able to write in zero gravity.

Today, ink is built into the design of most pens, although it is still possible to buy bottles and cartridges of ink. However, it was not always possible to buy ink in this way. Chinese ink, the oldest kind of ink, is made by combining soot with various other ingredients and is made in solid blocks. As the ink is needed, the block is rubbed gently on a stone with a little water and the ink is applied to paper with a special brush.

Fountain pens

These have their own supply of ink, often in special cartridges. They come in many different nib sizes.

Ball point pens

These are fountain pens with a tiny ball instead of a nib. *Replay pens* are a more recent development. They use ink which can be erased, but only within a couple of hours after writing. This kind of pen only works when you are writing on a flat surface.

Li T'ing–kuei's 10th Century recipe for ink

- 1⅓ pounds pine soot
- 3 oz ground mother of pearl
- 1 oz ground jade
- 1 oz Baroos camphor
- Raw lacquer

If available, add rhinoceros horn, pomegranate peel, gamboge, croton-oil bean and cinnabar.

Pound the mixture 100,000 times.

Handwriting

Have you ever thought about what an extraordinary thing handwriting is? Some people can produce beautiful handwriting almost without trying. Others are not so lucky. They have to put up with remarks that their writing looks as if a drunken spider has run across the page and other equally unhelpful comments.

Whether we like it or not, we all have to write in a way that other people can understand. And it's a fascinating thought that handwriting can probably tell us almost as much about the person who is writing as the words which appear on the paper.

The history of writing

Writing began over 20,000 years ago with paintings on cave walls which were probably intended to show other people what had happened in the hunt for food. The most well-known form of picture writing is possibly Egyptian hieroglyphics. Can you work out what each picture means?

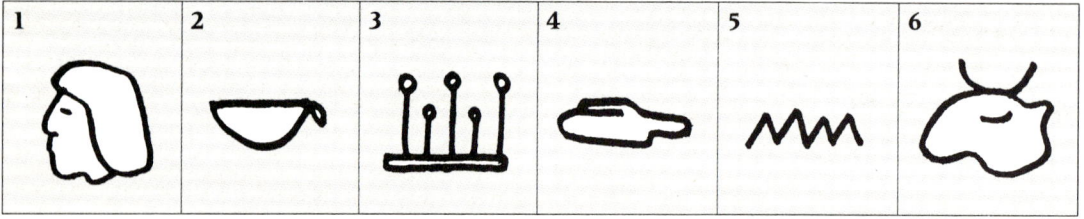

Answers: 1. head 2. vessel 3. field 4. hand 5. water 6. ox

Gradually these pictures evolved into *ideograms*, or symbols which represent ideas. Ideograms are still used today to form international road signs or to communicate important messages like 'No Smoking'.

Chinese writing uses ideograms which are usually known as characters. The Chinese people speak many different languages, but because their writing is based on ideograms and not individual sounds, the whole nation can use and understand the same books. Look at the diferent elements which make up the character for the words 'to listen'.

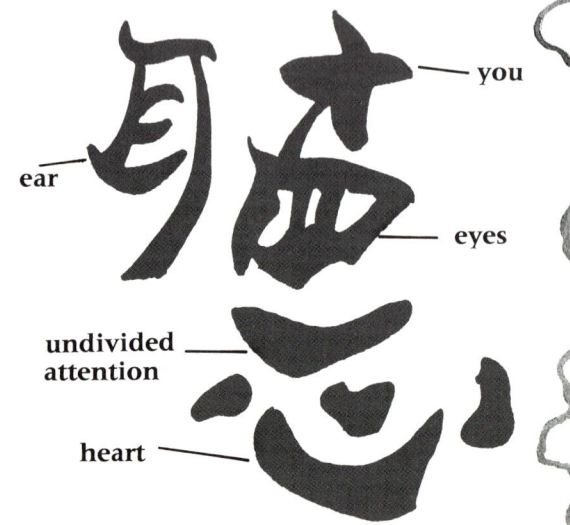

38

Ideographic writing has many advantages, but it also has some limitations. In order to be able to do the work set in a Chinese secondary school, you would need to know 3 500 different characters. Some of the characters are extremely complicated and need 50 or more separate marks with a pen or brush. It's hardly surprising that, in Hong Kong, primary school children are expected to spend an hour every day after school just practising their writing!

Alphabets, (from the first two letters of the Greek alphabet *alpha* and *beta*), represent sounds rather than ideas. This makes it possible to write any word using a fairly small number of letters and, of course, letters can be learned very quickly.

The first writing system to represent sounds was used nearly 5000 years ago by the Phoenicians, who lived in present-day Lebanon. The Phoenicians were a great sea-faring nation and carried their writing system to many different countries, where people changed it to suit the needs of their languages. The English language uses the Roman alphabet. The Romans had based their writing on the Greek alphabet which, in turn, had developed from Phoenician writing.

Today, many different alphabets are in common use. Do you recognise any of these examples?

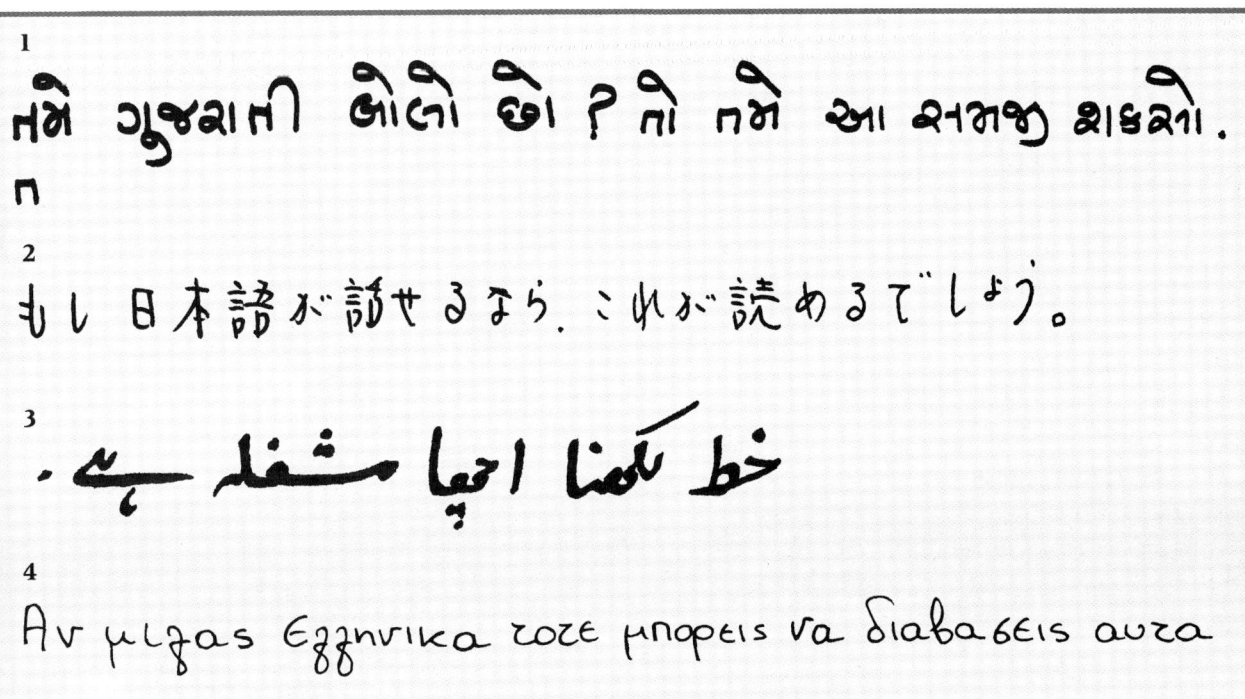

If you can speak 1. Gujarati, 2. Japanese, 3. Urdu and 4. Greek, you can read this!

What can handwriting tell you?

Handwriting is something very personal; each mark we make on a piece of paper is as individual as a section of a fingerprint. The way we each form letters is so distinctive that some people believe it is possible to tell personality from the way we write. It is certainly possible to detect a person's mental state from their handwriting. We write in a different way when we are upset or anxious than we do when we are calm and relaxed.

The study of handwriting has been developed into what some people claim to be a science called *graphology*. Take the many ways of writing the letter D. Do you form Ds like any of the examples below? And if so, is the description of your personality accurate?

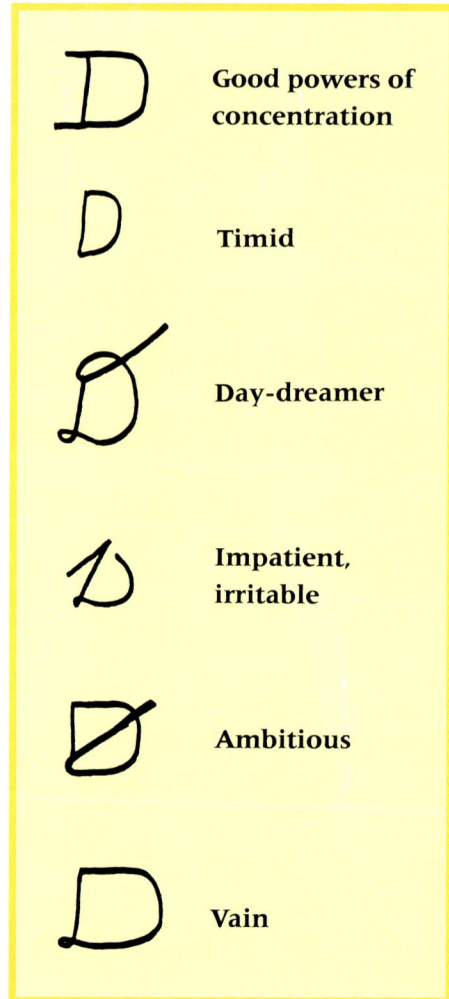

How old are you?

Even if you are not convinced about what graphology can tell you about your personality, there are many clues which any piece of writing can give you about the person behind the pen.

For instance, each generation has its own particular style of writing, and one of the things you notice when you look at old documents is just how much styles of writing have changed over the centuries, and how difficult they can be to decipher today.

The people who wrote the extracts below were born in 1553, 1738, 1897, 1946, 1975 and 1982. But can you tell which is which?

1 Look forward to seeing you soon. Hope you're well.

2 My dear friend most affectionately

3 Your friend and servant in God

4 I hope you are feeling better, and looking forward to

5 Best wishes fondest love Will Harrel

6 Once again thank you for the wonderful present.

Answers: 1. 1946 2. 1738 3. 1553 4. 1975 5. 1897 6. 1982

Which country do you come from?

Handwriting often differs from one country to another. British handwriting is different from American handwriting which, in turn, is different from French handwriting. Look at the sentences below. Children from Spain, Britain, the USA and Germany have each written *'Letter-writing is fun'*. Can you tell which sentence belongs to which child?

1 Letter writing is fun!

2 Letterwriding is Fun!

3 Letter writing is Fun

4 letter writing is fun

Answers: 1. USA 2. Germany 3. Britain 4. Spain

Printing

The printing press

Writing by hand can be very time consuming and for centuries people tried to mechanise the process. Printing with moveable type first began in China and Korea, but did not reach Europe until the fifteenth century. The first book printed in Europe is thought to have been a Bible produced in about 1455 on Johann Gutenberg's press in Germany.

Twenty years later, William Caxton was the first to print books in English. Printers, and later publishers, became very powerful people, deciding which forms of language were acceptable in print. In the fifteenth century, as today, many different dialects existed in Britain, but Caxton decided to use his own south eastern dialect. This is why, even today, it is rare to find books written in northern or southwestern or other dialects.

Printing made it possible to spread ideas and information quickly and cheaply. But in one way at least, it made life more difficult. Before printing, each word often had many different spellings. Once the presses were rolling, however, printers, dictionary makers and publishers decided that each word should have only one spelling.

There have been enormous developments in printing since Caxton's time, particularly in the second half of the twentieth century. If you'd like to find out more about printing, look through the list of books for further reading on page 48 of this book.

The first printed material was produced in the same way as this theatre poster. Ink was rolled over the raised surfaces of letters in a frame, or form. The form was then pressed against a sheet of paper.

Typewriters

The typewriter was invented in the United States in 1868 by Christopher Sholes and his colleagues. The first models only had capital letters. Have you ever wondered about the strange arrangement of letters on the keyboard? Wouldn't it seem more logical to put the letters in alphabetical order?

Early typewriters were difficult to operate and typing was a slow and tedious business. As the story goes, the designers decided to jumble the letters up to give the typist more of a challenge. The QWERTY keyboard [look at the first five letters of the first line] is still in use today, even though the human brain is so adaptable that, with a little training, we can learn to use even a QWERTY arrangement with great speed.

If you want to practice typing, why not type this sentence which uses all the letters of the alphabet.

Wordprocessors

Electrically-powered typewriters, which need less effort on the part of the typist, have been in use since about 1935. The most important recent development, though, has been the wordprocessing programs for personal computers. The computer stores what you type in its memory. It allows you to correct mistakes on the screen and to change the position of words, sentences or paragraphs. With certain computers, it is possible to use a range of fonts, or print styles and points, or type sizes.

The information keyed into a wordprocessor is usually printed out by one of three kinds of printer. A *letter quality* printer uses a 'golf ball' or sphere, covered with metal letters in the same way as an electric typewriter. The faster *dot matrix* printer builds up each character from tiny dots. A *laser* printer produces very high quality type quickly and silently.

Letters from history, history from letters

Letters can be a fascinating window on the past. They are very much like eyewitness accounts, helping us to share the excitement of great events or the sorrow of disasters. They can help us to understand what everyday life was like for people in the past – both the famous and the unknown.

Because history books often pay more attention to dates and events that to people, historical figures may seem stern, shadowy and very serious – not at all like real people. But the picture which we can build up from letters is often very different.

For example, have a look at this letter which Sir Henry Sydney wrote in 1566 to his son, Philip, who was at school in Shrewsbury. It tells us a great deal about what was expected of boys of twelve in the sixteenth century.

I have received two letters from you, one written in Latin, the other in French, which I take in good part. Exercise that practice of learning often; for that will stand you in good stead in that profession of life that you are born to live in.

Use moderate diet, so as after your meat you may find yourself fresher, and not duller, and your body more lively and not more heavy. Use exercise of body, but such as is without peril to your joints and your bones. It will increase your force, and enlarge your breath.

Above all things tell no untruth; the custom of it is naughty. For there can be no greater reproach to a gentleman, than to be accounted a liar.

Your loving father, so long as you live in the fear of God.

Mysteries of the past

History books are full of famous rulers, generals and politicians. But the past has also been shaped by ordinary people who did not become famous. These hidden histories are as important in their own way as the historical accounts of battles and elections.

Letters can play an important part in unravelling the past. In the early pioneer days in America, there were no newspapers, radio or television, but the letters that people wrote to friends and relatives they left behind give us important clues about what their life was like.

The Children's Museum in Indianapolis in the United States invites visitors to listen to a recording of a letter from Carolyn Marie Clark to her cousin, Anne. This letter gives a very clear picture of what it was like to live in a river settlement in the early nineteenth century.

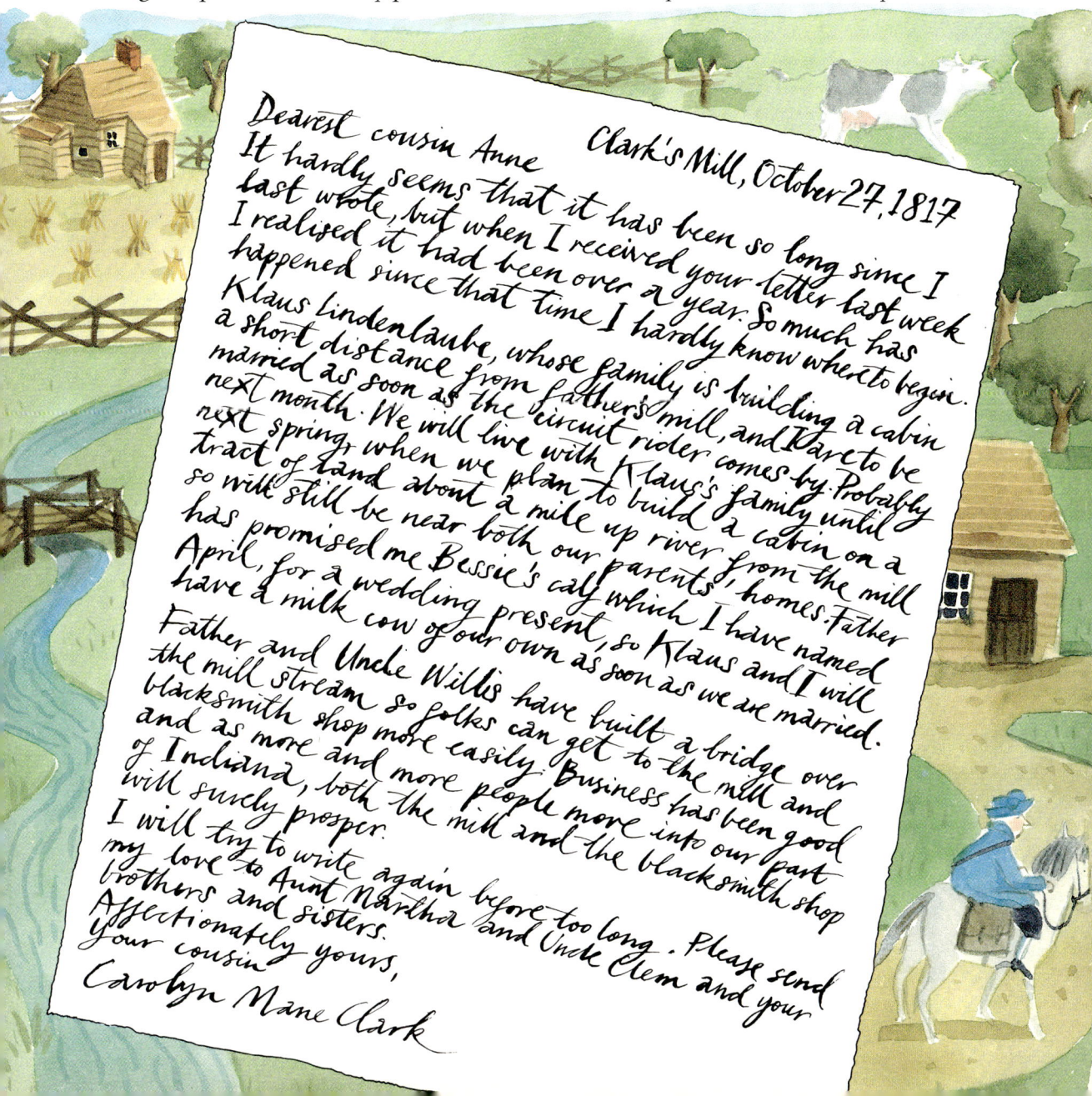

Clark's Mill, October 27, 1817

Dearest cousin Anne

It hardly seems that it has been so long since I last wrote, but when I received your letter last week I realised it had been over a year. So much has happened since that time I hardly know where to begin. Klaus Lindenlaube, whose family is building a cabin a short distance from father's mill, and I are to be married as soon as the circuit rider comes by. Probably next month. We will live with Klaus's family until next spring, when we plan to build a cabin on a tract of land about a mile up river from the mill so will still be near both our parents' homes. Father has promised me Bessie's calf which I have named April, for a wedding present, so Klaus and I will have a milk cow of our own as soon as we are married. Father and Uncle Willis have built a bridge over the mill stream so folks can get to the mill and blacksmith shop more easily. Business has been good and as more and more people move into our part of Indiana, both the mill and the blacksmith shop will surely prosper.

I will try to write again before too long. Please send my love to Aunt Martha and Uncle Clem and your brothers and sisters.

Affectionately yours,
Your cousin,
Carolyn Marie Clark

Family history

We all have our own family history. One way to find out about it is by asking parents and grandparents to tell us family stories which they can remember. Another way is to study documents like birth and marriage certificates or family bibles. But perhaps the most exciting way is to look at letters.

People often write letters when they leave home and are missing friends and relatives, or to share their sadness when somebody dies, or to say how happy thay are that a baby has been born or somebody is getting married. Because these are special letters, too precious to throw away, they are usually stored safely in a box or a drawer, often with the family photographs.

Letters can give you a glimpse of your own hidden history. Ask your parents, grandparents, aunts and uncles about any letters which they may have kept. And think about the letters which you write. What will your great-grandchildren think of you?

These relatives lived in East London.

A German relative.

Rachel with her family and friends before her journey to North America (Rachel is on the extreme right of the photograph.)

A letter from Rachel's sister.

David Wyman's family is Jewish. Some of them came to the East End of London from Poland and Germany at the beginning of the century. Many members of the family were killed in the holocaust in World War II. Messages on the back of photos and postcards, often in Hebrew, give David a feel for relatives he never met.

David doesn't know how these Polish relatives were related to him.

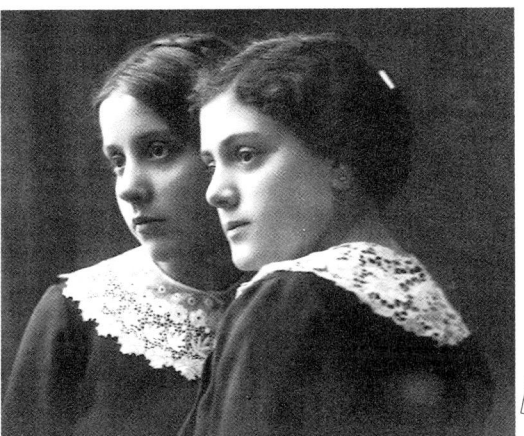

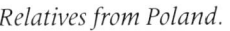

Relatives from Poland.   *A postcard written in Hebrew.*

Rachel's mother and father.

A letter from Rachel's mother.

Rachel Davies left South Wales for North America in 1929. She never saw her parents and sister again, so the letters they wrote to her were very special. As relatives in Britain and the United States read these letters today, they bring to life people scarcely remembered or known only through old photographs.

Index

addresses 21, 23, 24, 25
aerogrammes 30
air mail 19, 30
alphabets 39

cassette 5
collecting 28

design 3, 20, 21, 36

e-mail 35
envelopes 19, 24, 25, 28, 29, 31

family history 46, 47
fax machines 34
freebies 19
freepost 31
friends 4, 7, 20

graphology 40, 41
greeting cards 5, 26
handwriting 7, 36, 38, 40, 42
hieroglyphics 38
ideograms 38, 39
information 18, 19
ink 3, 7
invisible writing 15
invitations 3, 6
letter boxes 27, 30
letters:
 chain letters 13
 code letters 14, 15
 fan letters 3, 18
 formal letters 3, 20, 22, 23
 fun letters 3, 12, 21
 letters of complaint 17
 old letters 3, 41, 44, 45
 protest letters 16
 thankyou letters 3, 7

mirror writing 15
paper 3, 36
penfriends 3, 8, 9, 10, 11
pens 3, 36, 37
postcards 5, 12, 13, 27
postcodes 23, 25, 29
poste restante 31
postmark 24, 27, 28, 29
post office 19, 24, 31, 33
postscript 5
printing 42
relatives 4, 7, 20, 46
rough drafts 22
special occasions 5, 6
stamps 10, 19, 24, 27, 28, 29, 30, 31
surface mail 31
typewriter 7, 43
word processor 3, 7, 43
writing abroad 19, 30, 31

Useful addresses

Penfriends in the United Kingdom

International Friendship League, Penfriend Service UK, PO Box 117, Leicester, LE3 6EE

Send a stamped self-addressed envelope for information.

Penfriends in the European Community

Poste Europeene de l'Amitie, c/o Maison de l'Europe, 37 rue des Francs-Bourgeois, 75004 Paris, France

Penfriends worldwide

Australia

UNAA, International School Correspondence, Room 206, 147A King Street, Sydney, NSW 2000, Australia

Canada

Friends United Nations – FUN Club = 207, 11806 – 88th Avenue, Delta, BC, Canada V8C 305

New Zealand

Overseas Correspondance Department, United Nations Association of New Zealand, PO Box 1011, Wellington, New Zealand

United States

World Pen Pals, 1690 Como Avenue, St Paul, Minnesota 55108, USA

Enclose an international reply coupon for information.

Books for further reading:

Codes for Kids by Burton Albert Jr (Puffin)
Codes and Ciphers (Wayland)
Free Stuff for Kids by Maureen Maddren (Exley Publications)
Stamps! A Young Philatelist's Guide by Brenda Ralph Lewis (Simon and Schuster)
Stamps and Stamp Collecting (Usborne)
Lettering and Typography (Usborne)

Would you make a good penfriend?

Key to quiz on page 9:

a scores 3 points, **b** scores 2 points, **c** scores 1 point

16–21 You will make an excellent penfriend. You like letter-writing, you are interested in finding out about other people and places and probably have the staying power to make the correspondence last.

8–15 You will probably not be the world's most enthusiastic correspondent, but you could find writing to a penfriend a lot of fun just the same. Give it a try and you may well surprise yourself.

0–7 Penfriends are almost certainly not for you!

Answers to coded messages on Page 14:

3/15/4/5	12/5/20/20/5/18/19	18/21/12/5	15/11!
CODE	LETTERS	RULE	OK!
EMERGENCY	SUBJECT	BEING	TAILED
4□4464Ọ2?	57ị9426	ị48Ọ6	6Ọ8?43

P.S. In 1954, a young Scottish boy called Gordon Jarvie was interviewed by a journalist who was staying in the house next door. The interview was published in *Junior Scholastic*, a magazine read by Junior High School children all over the USA. In it Gordon said, 'I should like to have a few friends in America, and I hope some of you will write to me, though I cannot promise to answer every letter'. Little did he know how things were going to unfold!

Within a few weeks, letters were arriving by the sackful and the Jarvie's postman was beginning to get very upset. The post office complained that they simply could not cope with this volume of mail. Nor could Gordon and his family! In the next few months, they received an estimated 14,000 letters!

All the letters in this book have been written by real people but, to avoid a repetition of this kind of event, we have changed the addresses!